AN
EASY-READ
FACT
BOOK

Snakes

David Lambert

Franklin Watts

London   New York   Toronto   Sydney

© 1986 Franklin Watts Ltd

First published in Great Britain
   1986 by
Franklin Watts Ltd
12a Golden Square
London W1

First published in the USA by
Franklin Watts Inc.
387 Park Avenue South
New York
N.Y. 10016

UK ISBN: 0 86313 358 4
US ISBN: 0-531-10166-5
Library of Congress Catalog Card
   Number 85-51600

Designed and produced by
David Jefferis

Illustrated by
Drawing Attention
Eagle Artists
Hayward Art Group
Michael Roffe

Printed in Great Britain by
   Cambus Litho, East Kilbride

AN
EASY-READ
FACT
BOOK

Snakes

Contents

Anatomy of a snake

Snakes are long, thin, wriggly reptiles with no legs. Like other reptiles, such as crocodiles and lizards, snakes have backbones, dry scaly skin and need warmth to make them active.

Snakes probably got their strange shape from lizard ancestors that took to burrowing and so lost their need for arms and legs. In time, the limbs shrank and eventually disappeared. But snakes have very long, flexible backbones and scores of ribs. To fit inside this stream-lined body, kidneys are long and thin. Some snakes breathe with just one long lung instead of the usual pair.

On the outside, snakes are covered in scales, with a single wide row of scales under the belly.

Snakes have no earholes and no eyelids. Snakes cannot shut their eyes, but each eye is protected by a tough, transparent piece of skin called the spectacle.

▽ This snake skeleton shows the backbone is made of hundreds of interlocking bones called vertebrae. The ribs anchor muscles and protect internal organs. But there are no limb, hip or shoulder bones.

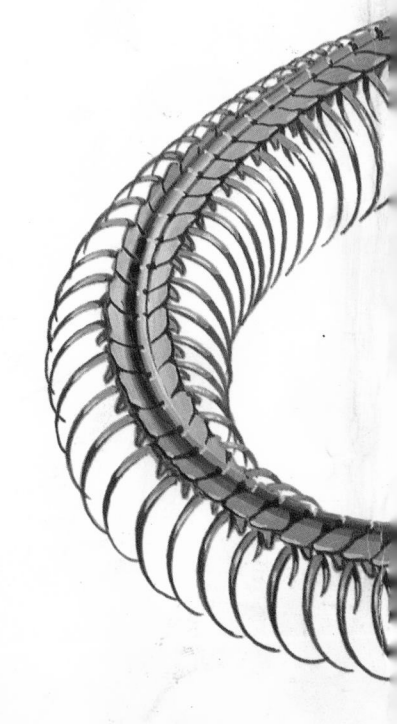

4

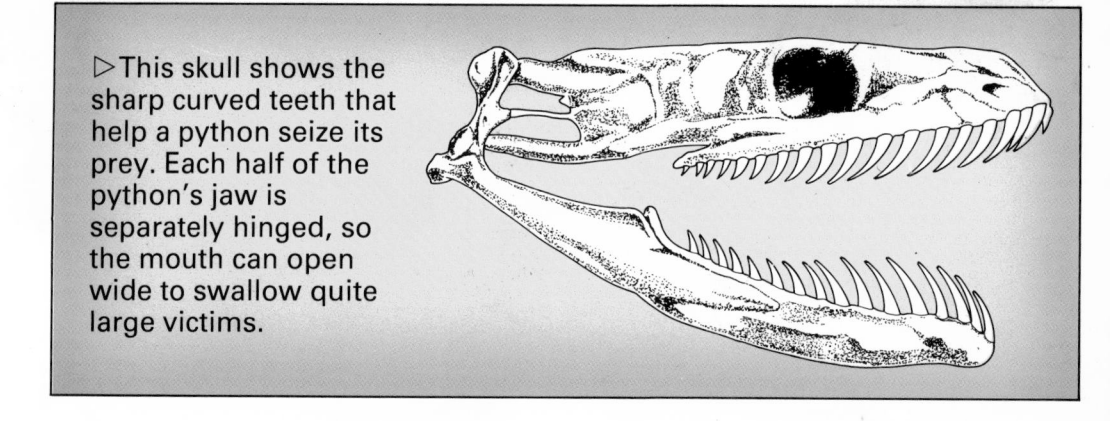

▷This skull shows the sharp curved teeth that help a python seize its prey. Each half of the python's jaw is separately hinged, so the mouth can open wide to swallow quite large victims.

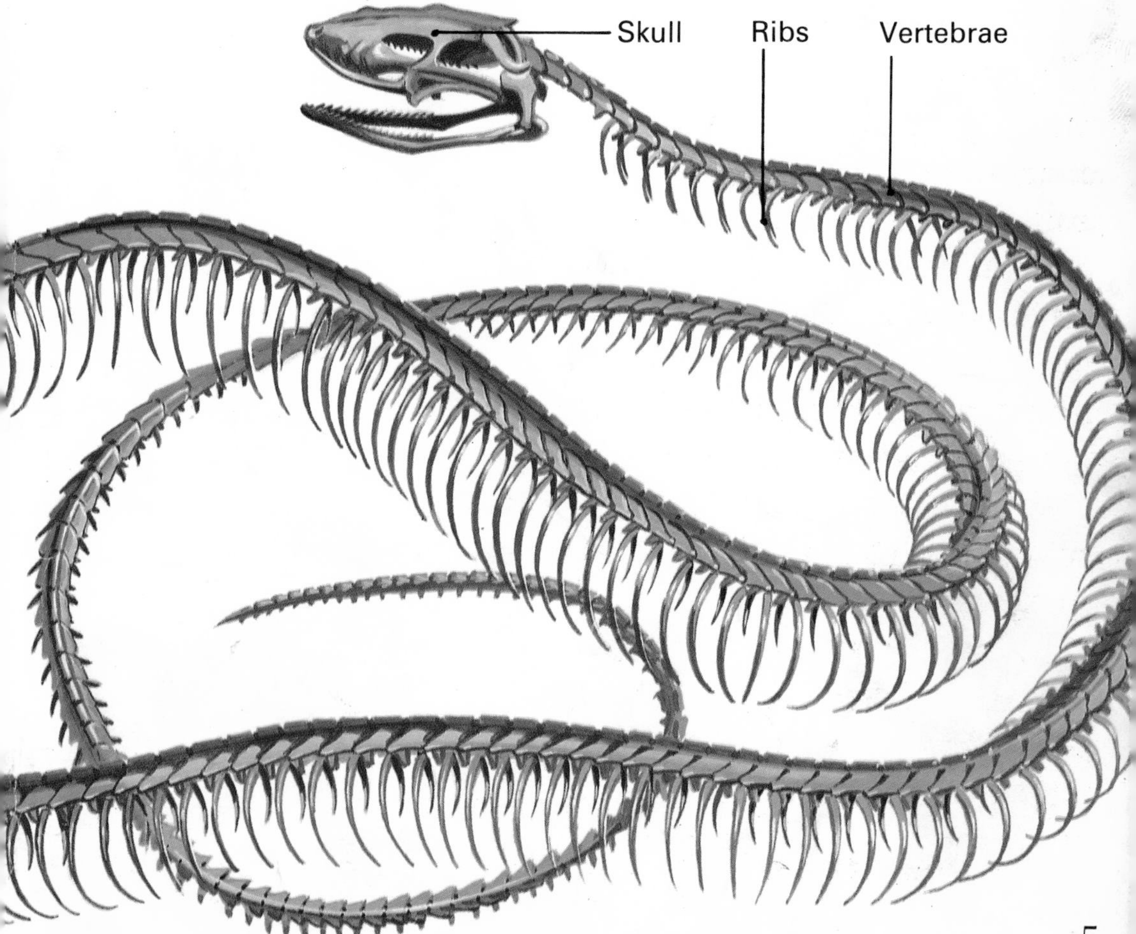

Skull   Ribs   Vertebrae

Wriggling snakes

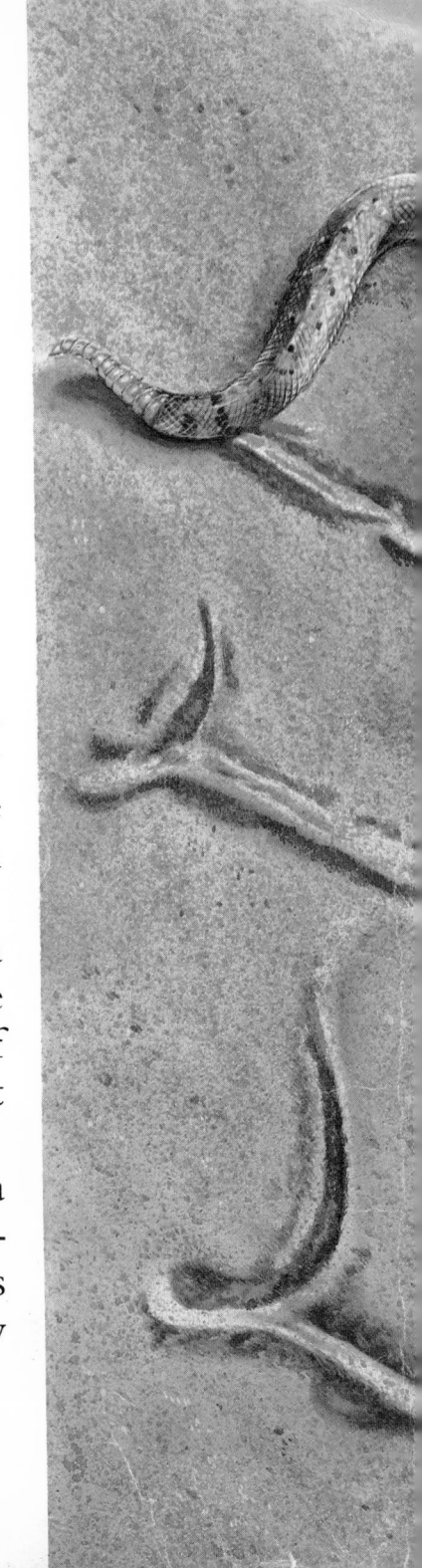

Snakes cannot run or walk, but they have no trouble moving about. To go forward, they press back against the ground under their bodies.

Most snakes wriggle along in a series of curves. As each body loop presses against the ground, part of the snake moves forward.

Some burrowing snakes use a kind of concertina movement. They throw their front end into loops that grip the sides of their burrow. Then they haul the tail-end toward the head.

Thick-bodied snakes may travel in a straight line, caterpillar fashion. The belly muscles bunch up in a series of waves to press back, in turn, against the ground.

The big picture on this page shows a desert snake "sidewinding." Rattlesnakes and vipers use this sideways motion to cross loose, hot sands. They leave tracks like the rungs of a ladder.

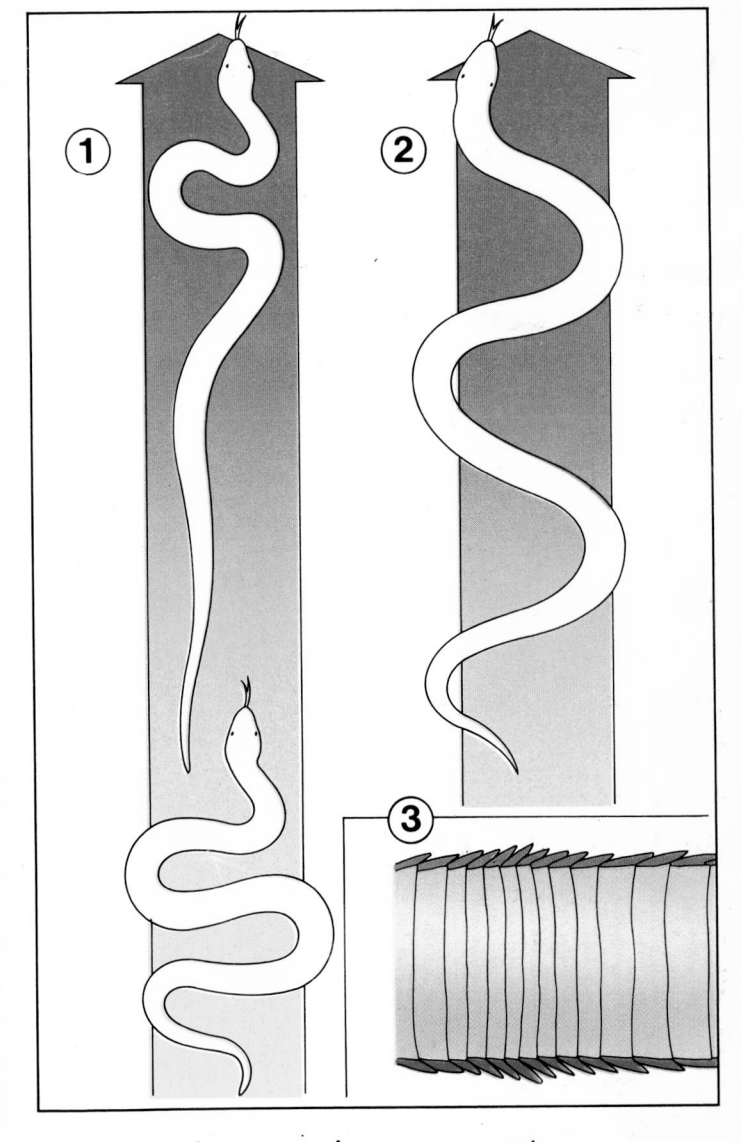

△ Here are three ways in which a snake may move.
1 Concertina movement.
2 Undulating movement.
3 Caterpillar crawl. Muscles bunch up to make belly scales (shown close-up) press back against the ground.

Snake senses

Senses help snakes to find food and avoid danger. But their eyes, ears and sense of smell are not quite like ours.

Most snakes probably see shape and color less clearly than we do, but they can spot the slightest movement.

Snakes have no external ears like ours and cannot hear airborne sounds. But they do have inner ears. These ears can detect ground vibrations, such as the quiet footsteps of an approaching rat.

Snakes have a good sense of smell. They also have a special organ that "tastes" tiny particles picked up by their forked tongues, from the air or on the ground.

All snakes have a good sense of balance and their skin can sense touch and warmth. Some also have heat sensors in front of their eyes so that they are able to track warm animals even at night.

▷ A banded rattlesnake sinks its fangs into a rat. The snake's heat-detecting pits – one in front of each eye – help it to close in on warm-blooded prey at night or in the darkness of a burrow.

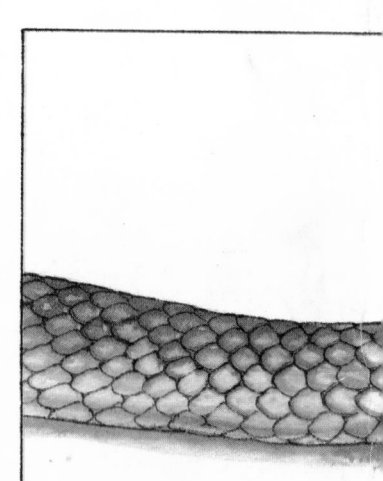

8

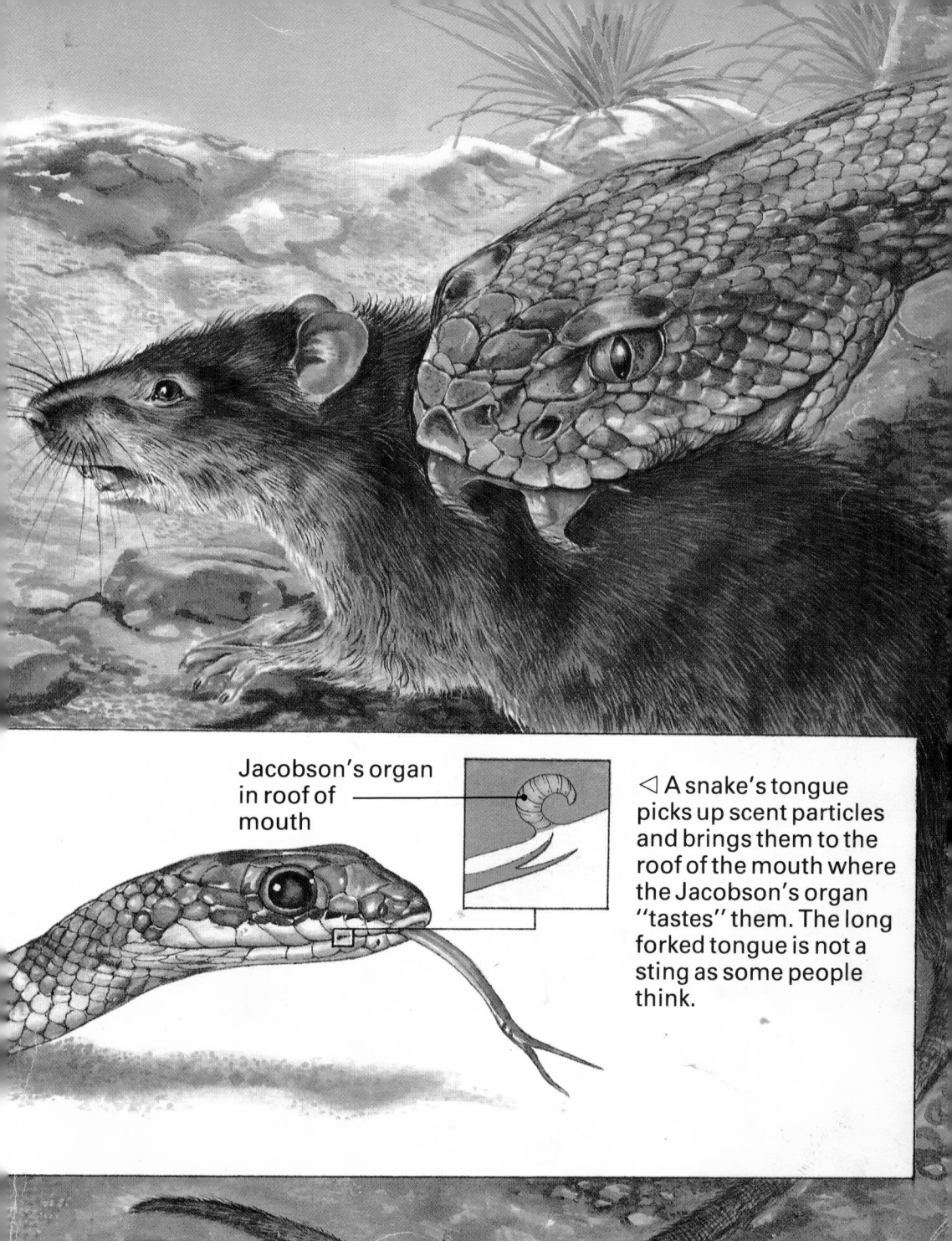

Jacobson's organ
in roof of
mouth

◁ A snake's tongue
picks up scent particles
and brings them to the
roof of the mouth where
the Jacobson's organ
"tastes" them. The long
forked tongue is not a
sting as some people
think.

Shedding skin

△ This diamondback rattlesnake shrugs off its dead, outer layer of skin, which bears the pattern of each scale. Revealed under the old skin is a new one that has grown to take its place. The old skin usually peels off in one, unbroken piece.

Tiny pieces of our outer skin flake off all the time as they wear out. But new skin is continuously growing underneath to replace the lost skin. Snakes also shed their old, dead outer skin, but they lose it as a single piece.

You can usually tell when a snake is getting ready to shed its skin, or molt. Its skin appears dull and cloudy, especially over the eyes. This is because a milky liquid collects between the old skin and the new one beneath. For a

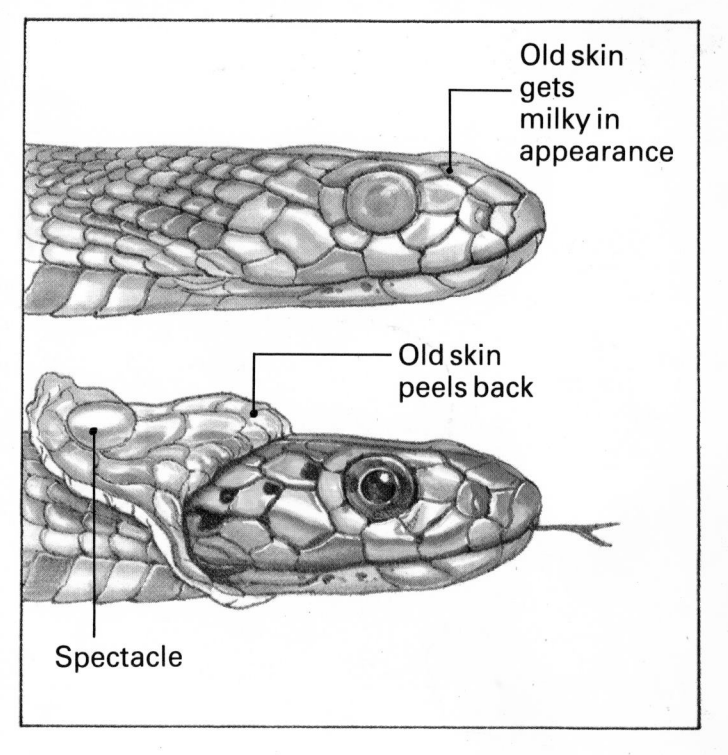

Old skin gets milky in appearance

Old skin peels back

Spectacle

few days, the snake may stop eating and hide. Then the cloudiness clears.

Next day, the snake may stretch its jaws and rub its mouth on a log or branch until its old skin splits open at the lips. As the snake goes on rubbing, the old skin peels off inside-out like a transparent fragile stocking.

The snake now has a bright new skin, a big appetite and becomes active again. But a few months later, it must shed its skin again.

△ The top snake's head looks milky because the skin will soon be shed. For a while, the snake is almost blind and hides.

Below, the old skin peels back, showing the spectacle which had been covering the snake's eye.

11

Hibernation

△ This snake has warmed up in the morning sun, so it can move about quickly and easily. If it gets too hot as the day goes on, it can move into the shade.

Snakes are cold-blooded. A snake's body is always as hot or cold as the air around it.

To warm up in the morning, a snake lies basking in the sun. If the snake gets too hot, it crawls into the shade. Most snakes live in lands with warm sunshine all year.

Some snakes live in cooler lands which have frost and snow in winter. As the autumn days get colder, a snake's body cools down too. It creeps

into a hole which is protected from the frost.

As the weather continues to get colder the snake's body gets colder and stiffer. Its heartbeat and breathing slow down and nearly stop. It falls into a deep winter "sleep" called hibernation.

Hibernating snakes use up so little energy that they live for months without a meal. When spring comes, they wake up and crawl out, rather thin and *very* hungry.

△ In winter, snakes hibernate in holes safe from the icy winds above. Sometimes many snakes share the same hibernating chamber. They may even share the space with small lizards or other creatures that they would normally hunt and eat.

13

Constrictors

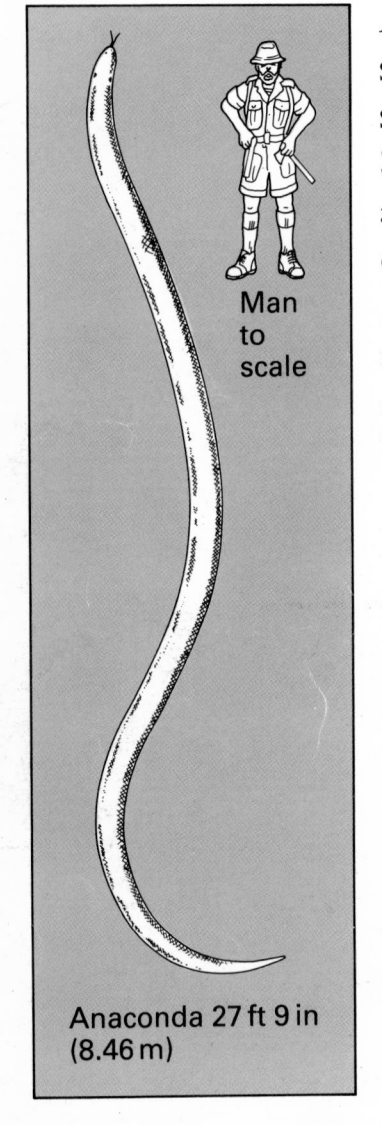

Man to scale

Anaconda 27 ft 9 in (8.46 m)

Almost all snakes catch living prey and swallow it whole. Many snakes simply seize a victim and gobble it down. Some snakes first coil themselves around their prey. These snakes are called constrictors.

Small constrictors, such as the smooth snake, may wrap two or three coils around a lizard to hold it still. Then they swallow it alive.

The great boas of America and the huge pythons of Africa, Asia and Australia behave differently. They kill their prey before they eat it. First they grip a creature with their teeth, then wrap themselves around its body and squeeze hard to stop it breathing. Then they swallow it whole.

◁ One of the longest anacondas, compared to a man. The snake measured 27 ft 9 in (8.46 m). It was shot in Brazil in 1962.

Anacondas are the world's bulkiest snakes and can attack even vicious river-dwelling caimans (crocodile-like animals).

Many giant constrictors eat animals no bigger than rats or chickens. Some though, will tackle antelopes or pigs. Anacondas and reticulated pythons – the largest snakes of all – can quite easily attempt to eat a human. Luckily, they seldom do!

Snakes sleep after large meals. After swallowing a pig, a python might not eat again for over a week.

▽ This boa constrictor coils itself tightly around its victim. There is little actual crushing in the kill. No bones are broken, but the victim cannot breathe and suffocates.

Danger! Poison

Some snakes kill with poison, known as venom. Snake venom is a kind of saliva, stored in glands in the head. Venomous snakes have hollow or grooved fangs. When the fangs puncture a victim's skin, venom squirts through the fangs.

There are four main types of poisonous snake. Each has a different type of fang arrangement.

Pit vipers, such as rattlesnakes, are those with heat-sensitive facial pits.

▽ This picture shows a cutaway through a rattlesnake's head. Poison, stored in sacs in the head, squirts through the hollow fangs like liquid from a doctor's syringe.

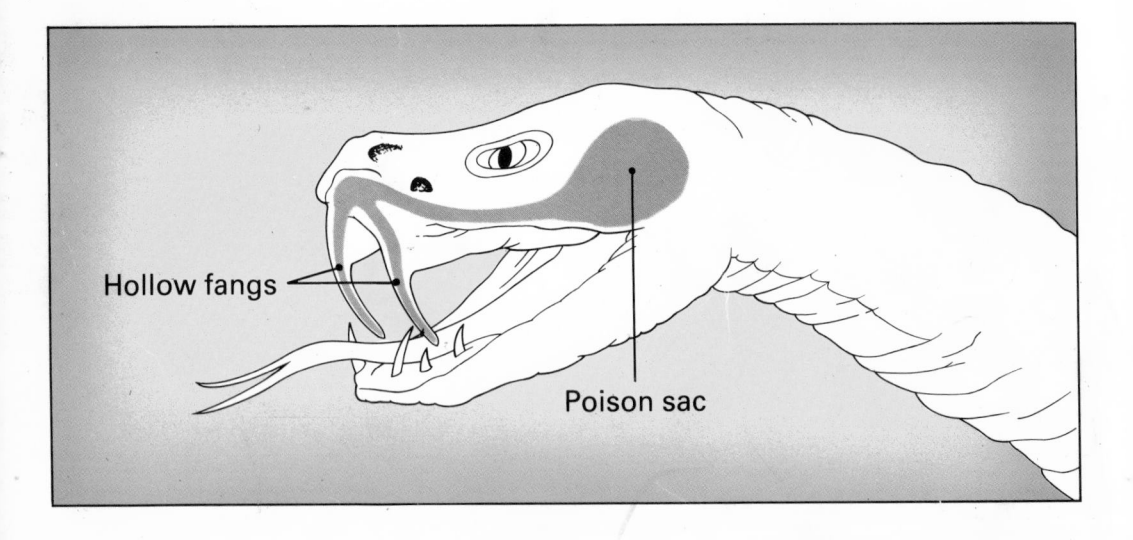

Hollow fangs

Poison sac

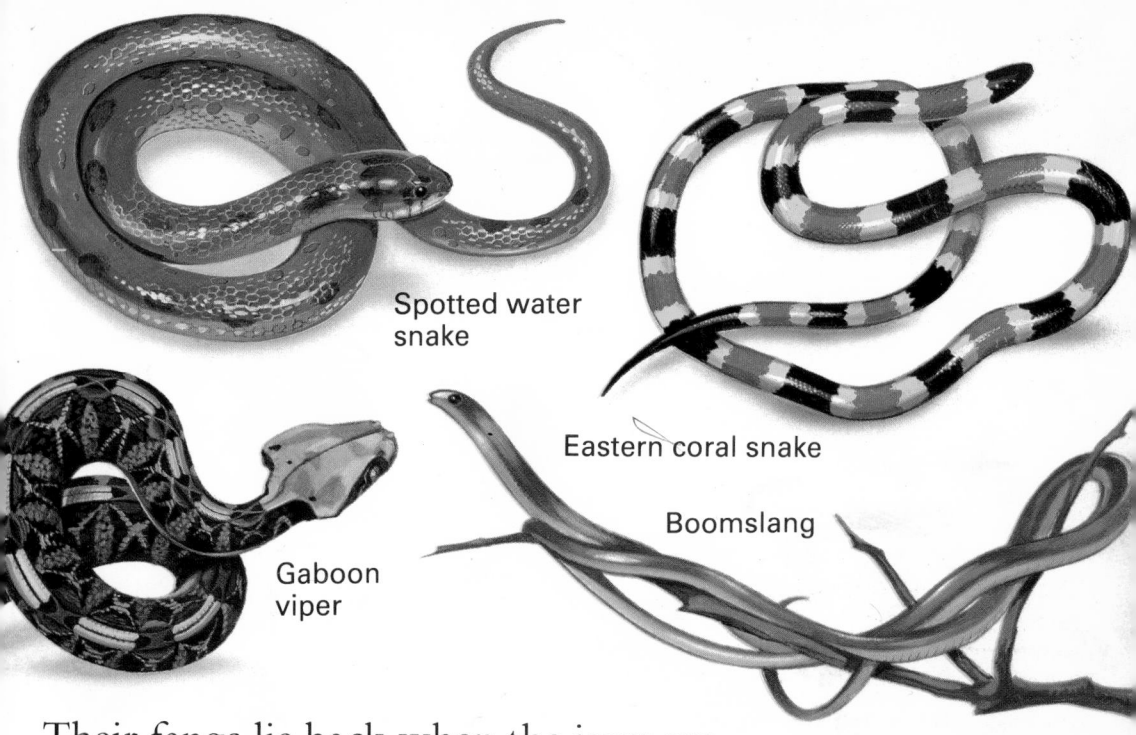

Spotted water snake

Eastern coral snake

Boomslang

Gaboon viper

Their fangs lie back when the jaws are shut, swinging forward as the jaws open. Adders and other vipers are mostly short fat snakes. They are also armed with long hinged fangs.

Cobras, coral snakes and mambas are members of the same group. They have fixed front fangs.

Back-fanged snakes, such as Africa's boomslang, squirt poison through short, grooved back teeth.

Some venomous snakes are deadlier than others, but only a few kinds are really dangerous to humans.

△ Here are four poisonous snakes. The spotted water snake and boomslang are back-fanged. The gaboon viper has long, hinged fangs. The coral snake has front fixed fangs.

Egg-eaters

Egg-eating snakes are small, harmless snakes. They can eat birds' eggs which are much bigger than their own jaws when wide open. Five types of egg-eaters live in Africa and one in India.

When feeding, the snake first flicks its tongue over an egg, to taste if it is good or bad. If the egg tastes good, the snake pushes it against a loop of its own body. It then works its mouth around the egg. The snake has no large teeth to get in the way. Even so, the task can take up to 20 minutes and the skin of the snake's mouth is stretched until it is as thin as paper.

Next, the egg moves into the throat, the snake arches its back and long, sharp spines, jutting from its backbone, press against the egg and break the shell. Then bony pegs crush the egg and the snake swallows the egg yolk and white. Afterwards the snake spits out the remnants of the crushed shell.

▷ Here you see an African egg-eating snake enjoying its supper.

Baby snakes

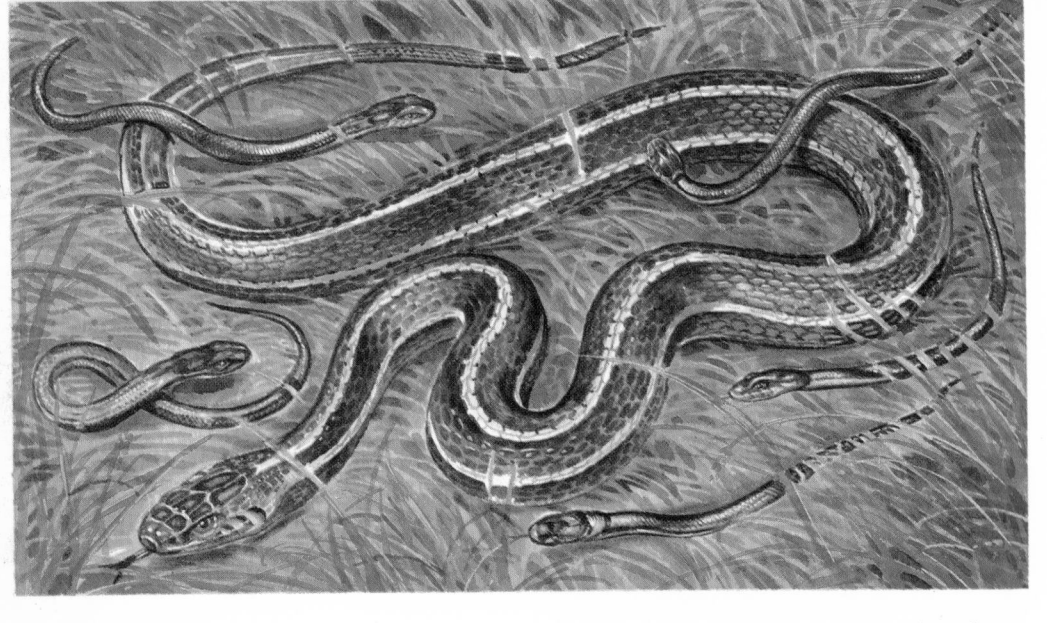

△ Garter snakes do not lay eggs. They give birth to a brood of 14 to 40 live young. A few mothers may guard their young for a few days, but soon the small creatures must find food for themselves.

Most snakes hatch from eggs laid on dry land. The eggs are covered by tough, white papery shells. A snake often lays her eggs – up to a hundred at a time – in a hole or crevice or in a heap of rotting vegetation. In most cases the mother snake wriggles away after laying the eggs.

Some snakes though, including certain pythons, stay on guard. Either way, heat from the Sun or rotting leaves cause the eggs to hatch.

Baby snakes emerge from the eggs days or even months after they were laid, depending on the temperature. Each snake has a special tooth to help it cut its way out through the shell.

Not all snakes start life like this. Boas and many kinds of vipers hatch from eggs as they are being laid.

Whichever way they hatch, life for young snakes is very dangerous. All kinds of animals, from frogs to birds, hunt them down.

△ This reticulated python lays between eight and 100 eggs. She pushes them into a heap, coils around them and guards them for months until they hatch.

Snake enemies

△ The Indian mongoose kills cobras and other deadly snakes. The mongoose darts in and bites the snake's neck or jaw so it cannot strike back. Even if a mongoose is bitten, it may survive – its body resists venom extremely well.

From the moment they hatch, snakes face many enemies. A young snake may be snapped up by a frog. Even the largest snakes may be attacked.

Two otters once killed an Indian python measuring 17 ft (5.2 m), and people have found half-eaten remains of pythons inside hyenas, tigers and crocodiles.

Most small flesh-eating mammals enjoy a snake snack. Hedgehogs and mongooses kill snakes by biting. Pigs

trample snakes with their horny feet. Hawks and other birds attack by tearing with their claws and beaks.

All these animals must be nimble to avoid a deadly bite. But king snakes seem immune to the poison of the rattlesnakes they eat.

Human beings are snakes' worst enemies. Some people kill any snake, however harmless it is. Builders and farmers often destroy the wild places where snakes live.

△ This secretary bird grips a snake in its beak. These tall, long-legged birds roam African grasslands, stamping to flush out prey. They kill large snakes by trampling them and spread their wings as shields against snakebites.

Snakes of the world

Here are some of the estimated 2,700 species of snakes. They vary in length from a few inches to many feet.

1 Puff adders are big, thick African vipers that puff themselves up when alarmed.
2 The elephant trunk snake of Malaysia is a water snake.
3 The common garter snake of North America eats worms, frogs and fish.
4 The taipan from New Guinea and Australia is one of the world's most poisonous snakes.
5 The grass snake is also known as the smooth green snake. It may hiss and strike, but seldom bites.
6 The gopher snake kills rodents that harm crops. It lives all across North America.
7 Dark green whip snakes prey on small mammals in dry parts of southeast Europe.

1 Puff adder

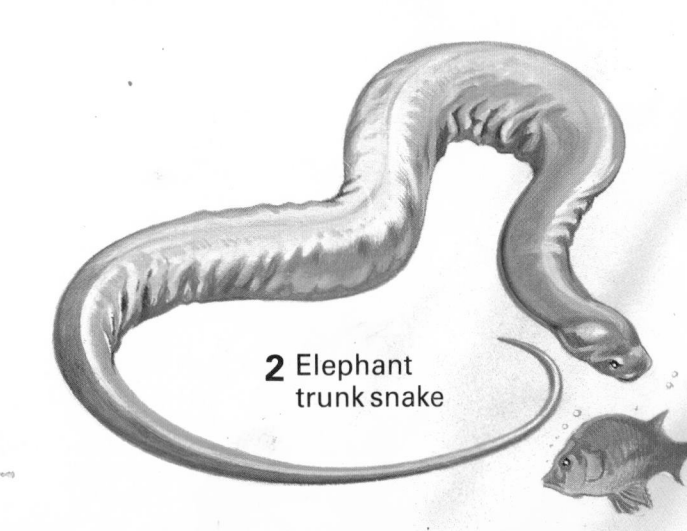

2 Elephant trunk snake

4 Taipan

5 Grass snake

3 Common garter snake

6 Gopher snake

7 Dark green whip snake

Snakes of the world

1 Western
blind snake

2
Indian
python

Indian cobra
4

3 Anaconda

5
Banded
sea snake

6 Asp viper

7 Common viper (adder)

8 Bushmaster

9 Eastern diamond rattlesnake

1 The western blind snake is from the southwestern United States.

2 Indian pythons spend much time in trees, in forests from India to Indonesia. Some grow as big as 20 ft (6 m).

3 Anacondas include some of the longest and heaviest snakes. They live in the rivers of South America.

4 Indian cobras rear up and spread their necks to frighten enemies. Then they strike with poisonous fangs.

5 Banded sea snakes live in warm seas. They swim with flattened, oar-like tails and kill fish with venom.

6 Asp vipers live in France and Italy. They are more poisonous than adders.

7 Common vipers, also known as adders, are poisonous snakes that live in Europe and northern Asia.

8 South America's bushmaster is the longest poisonous snake in the Americas at 12 ft (3.6 m) or more.

9 Eastern diamondback rattlesnakes live in the southeastern United States.

27

Keeping snakes

△ This anaconda is in a zoo cage. Zoos can provide even the largest snakes with plenty of room to bask and bathe. However, many big snakes seem happy in quite small enclosures.

A harmless snake can make an interesting pet if cared for properly.

Most snakes thrive best in cages that are kept completely dry except for drinking water. An all-glass aquarium makes a suitable container. Cover the floor with sheets of newspaper. For a sleeping den add a cardboard box with a hole cut in one side. When the snake is inside, you can lift out the box to clean the tank. Make sure you seal the top, or the snake will escape. In one corner of

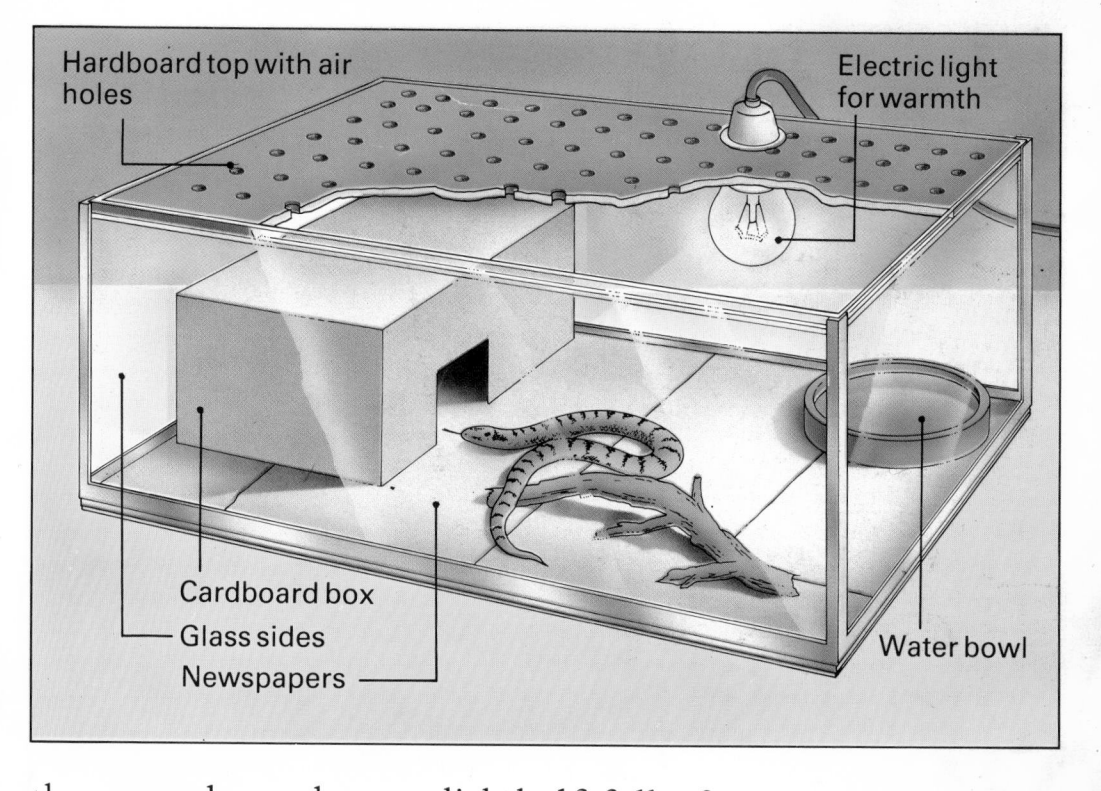

Hardboard top with air holes

Electric light for warmth

Cardboard box

Glass sides

Newspapers

Water bowl

the cage place a heavy dish half-full of drinking water and change this often. Also, some snakes might like a branch to climb on.

Add a firmly fitting hardboard lid with many air holes and wire mesh. Arrange a light bulb so that it heats one end of the tank to about 79°F (26°C).

Find out what food your snake will eat and how often it should have a meal. Most snakes learn to eat dead mice or fish.

△ A cage equipped like this suits most small snakes. A dry floor reduces the danger of disease and smooth sides prevent injuries.

Glossary

Here are explanations of some of the words used in this book.

Back-fanged snakes
Venomous snakes with poisonous fangs at the back of the mouth. They include the boomslang snake of Africa.

Boas
A family of big constrictors of tropical America. Among the boas is the anaconda, probably the bulkiest of snakes.

Cold-blooded
Animals whose body temperature is the same as the air around them. Cold-blooded creatures include snakes and lizards. Warm-blooded animals have bodies which maintain the same temperature regardless of the weather. Humans stay at 98.4°F (37°C). If it is hot, we sweat to cool off; if it is cold we burn food energy to keep warm.

Constrictor
Snake that coils around its prey to suffocate it or hold it still while it is swallowed.

Egg-eating snakes
Snakes which swallow, crush and eat sizable eggs. Egg-eaters have projections under their backbones which stick down to break the eggshells.

Fangs
Long, sharp stabbing teeth. Venomous snakes have either hollow or grooved fangs through which they squirt poison.

Hibernation
A kind of deep winter sleep.

Jacobson's organ
A pair of tiny scent "tasting" pits in the roof of a snake's mouth.

Molt
To shed skin.

Pit vipers
Rattlesnakes and some other venomous snakes. They have two small pits on their heads, in front of their eyes. These are sensitive heat detectors – a rattlesnake can find its prey using them, even in the dark.

Pythons
Large constrictor snakes found in Asia, Africa and Australia.

Reptiles
Cold blooded animals with dry, scaly skin and a backbone. They include animals such as crocodiles.

Scales
Hard, flat plates covering the bodies of reptiles and fish.

Venom
Poison, a special kind of saliva, made in a snake's body.

Vipers
Venomous group of mostly short, thick snakes including the adder.

30

Snake facts

The page reveals some strange facts about snakes and the way they live.

Longest snake
The longest accurately measured snake is probably one that was shot in Indonesia in 1912. It was a reticulated python which measured 32 ft 9½ in (10 m).

Shortest snake
Full-grown thread snakes from the West Indies can be shorter than a man's hand — under 6½ in (17 cm).

Longest hibernation
Adders in the far north of Europe hibernate for up to nine months of each year.

Fastest snake
The poisonous black mamba of Africa can reach about 10 mph (16 km/h) when moving downhill. This is about as fast as a man jogging.

▽ A warning rattle
Rattlesnakes warn off enemies by shaking a rattle at the end of the tail. One scale is added to the rattle each time the snake sheds its skin.

Most deadly snake
The venom from some sea snakes is 100 times more poisonous than any land snake's venom.

Large families
Some snakes produce large broods. Russell's viper can give birth to 60 live young. Pythons lay over 100 eggs.

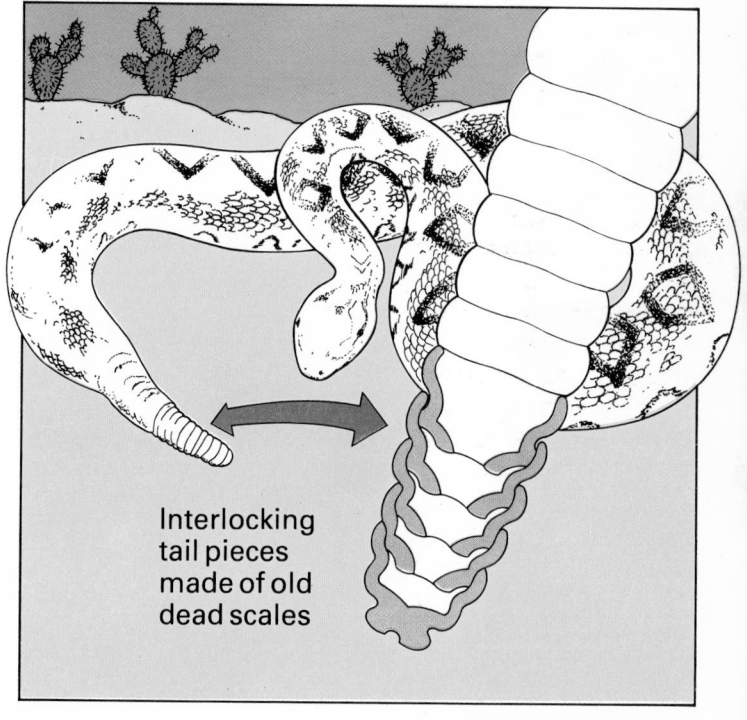

Interlocking tail pieces made of old dead scales

Index